A Note from
Mary Pope Osborne About the

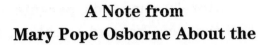

When I write Magic Tree House® adventures, I love including facts about the times and places Jack and Annie visit. But when readers finish these adventures, I want them to learn even more. So that's why we write a series of nonfiction books that are companions to the fiction titles in the Magic Tree House® series. We call these books Fact Trackers because we love to track the facts! Whether we're researching dinosaurs, pyramids, Pilgrims, sea monsters, or cobras, we're always amazed at how wondrous and surprising the real world is. We want you to experience the same wonder we do—so get out your pencils and notebooks and hit the trail with us. You can be a Magic Tree House® Fact Tracker, too!

Mary Pope Osborne

Here's what kids, parents, and teachers have to say about the Magic Tree House® Fact Trackers:

"They are so good. I can't wait for the next one. All I can say for now is prepare to be amazed!" —Alexander N.

"I have read every Magic Tree House book there is. The [Fact Trackers] are a thrilling way to get more information about the special events in the story." —John R.

"These are fascinating nonfiction books that enhance the magical time-traveling adventures of Jack and Annie. I love these books, especially *American Revolution*. I was learning so much, and I didn't even know it!" —Tori Beth S.

"[They] are an excellent 'behind-the-scenes' look at what the [Magic Tree House fiction] has started in your imagination! You can't buy one without the other; they are such a complement to one another." —Erika N., mom

"Magic Tree House [Fact Trackers] took my children on a journey from Frog Creek, Pennsylvania, to so many significant historical events! The detailed manuals are a remarkable addition to the classic fiction Magic Tree House books we adore!" —Jenny S., mom

"[They] are very useful tools in my classroom, as they allow for students to be part of the planning process. Together, we find facts in the [Fact Trackers] to extend the learning introduced in the fictional companions. Researching and planning classroom activities, such as our class Olympics based on facts found in *Ancient Greece and the Olympics*, help create a genuine love for learning!" —Paula H., teacher

MAGIC TREE HOUSE® FACT TRACKER

Llamas and the Andes

A NONFICTION COMPANION TO MAGIC TREE HOUSE #34:
Late Lunch with Llamas

BY MARY POPE OSBORNE
AND NATALIE POPE BOYCE

ILLUSTRATED BY ISIDRE MONÉS

A STEPPING STONE BOOK™

Random House 🏠 New York

Text copyright © 2020 by Mary Pope Osborne and Natalie Pope Boyce
Interior illustrations copyright © 2020 by Penguin Random House LLC
Cover photograph by mcjeff/shutterstock, used under license from Shutterstock

The Magic Tree House Fact Tracker series was formerly known as the Magic Tree
House Research Guide series.

Visit us on the Web!
MagicTreeHouse.com
rhcbooks.com

Educators and librarians, for a variety of teaching tools, visit us at
RHTeachersLibrarians.com

Library of Congress Cataloging-in-Publication Data
Names: Osborne, Mary Pope, author. | Boyce, Natalie Pope, author. | Monés, Isidre,
illustrator.
Title: Llamas and the Andes: a nonfiction companion to Magic Tree House #34,
late lunch with llamas / by Mary Pope Osborne and Natalie Pope Boyce; illustrated by
Isidre Monés.
Description: New York: Random House Children's Books, [2020] | Series: Magic Tree
House fact tracker | "A Stepping Stone book." | Includes bibliographical references
and index.
Identifiers: LCCN 2019029714 | ISBN 978-1-9848-9323-9 (paperback) |
ISBN 978-1-9848-9324-6 (lib. bdg.) | ISBN 978-1-9848-9325-3 (ebook)
Subjects: LCSH: Llamas—Andes—Juvenile literature. | Animals—Andes—Juvenile
literature. | Incas—Juvenile literature. | Andes—History—Juvenile literature.
Classification: LCC SF401.L6 O83 2020 | DDC 636.2/966—dc23

Printed in the United States of America

10 9 8 7 6 5 4 3 2 1

This book has been officially leveled by using the F&P Text Level Gradient™
Leveling System.

For Ben Corbett and Emily Kasten

Historical Consultant:
R. ALAN COVEY, PhD, Department of Anthropology, University of Texas at Austin

Scientific Consultant:
DEEANN M. REEDER, PhD, Department of Biology, Bucknell University

Education Consultant:
HEIDI JOHNSON, language acquisition and science education specialist, Bisbee, Arizona

Special thanks to the Random House team: Mallory Loehr, Jenna Lettice, Isidre Monés, Polo Orozco, Jason Zamajtuk, and endless thanks to Diane Landolf, who is the best editor anywhere

Llamas and the Andes

Contents

Dear Readers,

In <u>Late Lunch with Llamas</u>, we rescued a baby llama named Cria, who belonged to a boy in the Andes Mountains. We learned a lot about llamas and the Andes.

Did you know that the Andes are the second-tallest mountain range in the world? They run through parts of South America for about 4,500 miles.

Llamas have been an important part of life in the Andes for thousands of years. In fact, people in the Andes probably wouldn't have survived without them. Llamas carried heavy loads up

and down the mountains for them and still do today. This is just one important way that llamas helped them, but there are many, many more!

So let's put on our hiking boots and head for the Andes. You won't believe all the fantastic sights you'll see there!

Jack

Annie

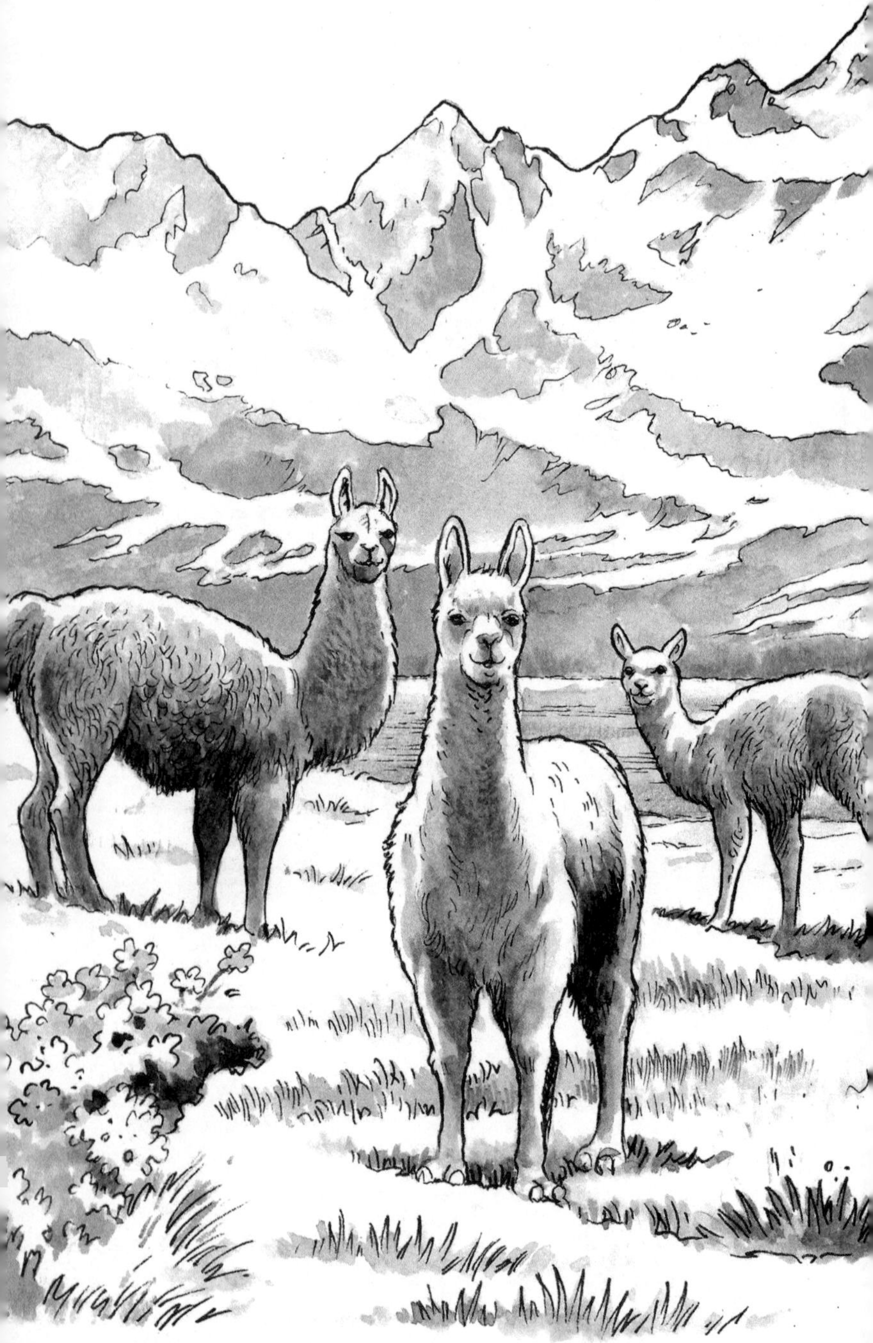

1

Llamas and the Andes

It's hard to think of the Andes Mountains without llamas (LAH-muzz). People have raised them in these spectacular mountains for thousands of years. Today llamas are all over the world, but millions still live high in the Andes.

The Andes are a chain of mountains stretching along the western coast of South America. They cover about 4,500 miles

through seven countries: Argentina, Bolivia, Chile, Colombia, Ecuador, Peru, and Venezuela.

The tallest mountain in the chain is Aconcagua (ah-kon-KAH-gwah), at 22,841 feet.

The Andes began forming about 30 million years ago. They are the longest mountain range in the world and in some places are over 400 miles wide! Except for the Himalayas, they are also the highest. These beautiful mountains have different kinds of weather and landforms. There are deep valleys, high deserts, flat plains, and snowcapped peaks.

There are three major regions in the Andes. The southern section is in Argentina and Chile. The central Andes run through parts of Chile, Bolivia, and Peru. And the northern Andes are in Venezuela, Colombia, and Ecuador.

 The Ojos (OH-hohs) del Salado is over 22,000 feet high and is one of 150 active volcanoes in the Andes.

The southern region is rainy and cool, but the central region is dry. There's rain in the north, but because it's closer to the equator, the temperatures there are warm.

Glaciers

The Andes have deserts, but they also have glaciers. Some on the border of Argentina and Chile look like icy rivers. For thousands of years, the glaciers have inched down the mountains, carving out valleys and high, flat plains as they go.

Plains like this one in Peru are large, flat areas of land.

Every year, water from the glaciers flows east into the Amazon River. The river begins high in the mountains of Peru and runs over 4,000 miles through the Amazon rain forest into the Atlantic Ocean.

The Nile, in Africa, is the only river that is longer than the Amazon.

Cloud Forests

There are rain forests in the Andes. And high in the mountains of Colombia, Ecuador, and Peru are cloud forests, where the trees are always covered in clouds.

Cloud forests form when warm, wet air from the Amazon rain forest moves up the mountains. The air cools as it gets higher and then condenses, or changes into clouds.

Trees in a misty cloud forest look like something from a fairy tale. Drops of

This cloud forest is part of Manú
National Park, in Peru.

water called *fog drip* trickle down to the
ground from the leaves. The earth is so
damp that soft mosses thrive on the dark
forest floor.

**Plants and Animals of the Cloud
Forest**

Many unusual animals and plants live in
Andean cloud forests. People have spotted over 300 different kinds of birds.

19

Animals such as the spectacled bear, long-whiskered owlet, and yellow-tailed woolly monkey are just some of the fascinating and rare creatures living in the cloud forests.

Mountain tapirs are relatives of horses and rhinos.

Different kinds of ferns, including tree ferns, are everywhere. Thousands of colorful orchids and many other plant species also thrive in this beautiful world of fog, trees, and waterfalls.

Other Plants in the Andes

There are 30,000 to 40,000 species of plants in the Andes! Cacti, orchids, and twenty-foot aloe plants are just a few of them.

There are 200 different kinds of orchids in the cloud forests.

21

The *Cinchona* (sin-CHO-nuh) is a small but very important tree. People grind up its bark to make *quinine* (KWY-nine), a medicine that treats people with *malaria* all over the world.

There are strange and wonderful plants like the *frailejones* (fry-lay-HOH-nezz) in Colombia. They look like small palm trees.

Frailejones are in the sunflower family.

And if you like ferns, there are 1,500 different kinds. And 1,200 kinds of moss!

Minerals

The Andes are rich in minerals. In fact, they have some of the largest deposits of copper, silver, tin, zinc, and gold in the world. The first explorers from Spain were there to mine for gold and other minerals.

Spanish explorers arrived in the Andes in the early 1500s.

People are still mining today. Chile has the largest gold mines in South America. Experts think there are at least 13,000 tons of gold yet to be found!

Breathing in the Thin Air

Because the Andes are so high, breathing can be difficult. At above 8,000 feet, the air doesn't hold much oxygen. Gravity pulls the oxygen down toward the earth's surface.

Without enough oxygen, people can get headaches and feel very tired. They might be dizzy and sick to their stomachs. If they become short of breath, it's important to get to a lower altitude as soon as possible.

24

Mountain climbers move slowly up the mountains so their bodies can adjust to the lack of oxygen.

Native people in the Andes have adapted to handle the lack of oxygen. Their red blood cells are larger and hold more oxygen than most other people's. They have larger chests, hearts, and lungs so they can breathe more deeply.

Whales in the Desert!

The Atacama Desert lies along the western edge of the Andes. In 2011, men working on a road there uncovered some strange bones ... a lot of them! Scientists visited the site and found they were the fossils of whales and other sea creatures. They were about 5 million years old!

Researchers wanted to know how these fossils got so far from the ocean. They discovered that whole groups of animals probably died from eating toxic algae.

Their dead bodies washed up onshore and lay buried in sand. Over the years, the bones became fossils. As the mountains grew higher, they pushed the fossils up about 130 feet, and they wound up in the Atacama Desert!

2

![llama silhouette]

Llamas

Llamas are *camelids*, meaning they come from the camel family. Camelids first appeared in North America millions of years ago.

Today relatives of these early camels live in Africa and Asia.

About 2 million to 3 million years ago, some camelids crossed a land bridge that linked North America to Europe and Asia.

As some camelids were crossing the

land bridge, others began to make their way down to South America. Llamas, alpacas, guanacos, and vicuñas come from this group.

The Four Camelids of the Andes

There are four kinds of camelids that live in the Andes: guanacos, vicuñas, llamas, and alpacas. They are all adapted to live high in the mountains. Their chests, hearts, and lungs are large. They have more red blood cells than other animals. Their thick coats keep them warm in the cold mountain air.

The vicuña is the national animal of Peru.

Llamas and Alpacas

Guanacos and vicuñas are wild animals. But over 6,000 years ago, people in the Andes began taming some of them. Over time, those became llamas and alpacas. Llamas come from guanacos, and alpacas come from vicuñas. People grew to depend on these animals for survival.

Llamas can carry 50 to 75 pounds. Alpacas are not strong enough to carry heavy loads.

Early people in the Andes had not yet invented the wheel. They carried things from one place to another on their backs. Some of them realized that they could train llamas as pack animals to carry their heavy loads.

The native people made their clothes, blankets, ropes, and rugs from llama and alpaca wool. Their sturdy leather sandals came from llama hides. Llama and alpaca meat added protein to their diets.

People in South America still eat llama meat.

31

Llama fat was made into candles.

Andeans dried llama and alpaca dung and burned it in fires for cooking and warmth. The dung also made excellent fertilizer that helped crops grow well in the poor mountain soil. Llama and alpaca dung is especially good fertilizer for growing corn at very high altitudes.

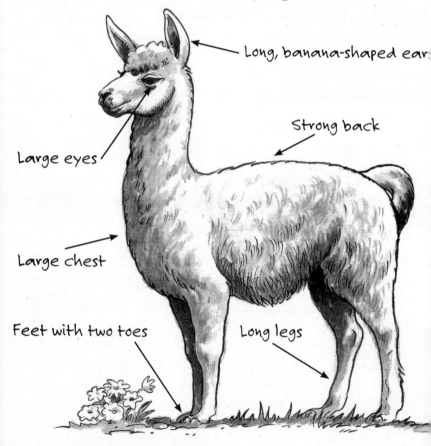

Long, banana-shaped ear

Strong back

Large eyes

Large chest

Feet with two toes

Long legs

How to Spot a Llama

Llamas can be over six feet tall and weigh about 400 pounds. Their long, banana-shaped ears stand straight up, and their hearing is excellent.

Many predators have eyes that focus straight ahead. Animals that are their prey, such as llamas, often have wide-set eyes. Large eyes on either side of their head give llamas a wide view of what's happening around them.

Llamas come in different colors. The most common are brown with yellow or white spots, but they can also be black, gray, and white.

Llama wool is tough and strong. It's great for making rugs, warm clothes, blankets, and ropes.

 Llamas in the Andes are usually sheared, or shaved, once a year.

Great Feet!

Like most animals living in the mountains, llamas have special ways of dealing with the environment. They are able to move easily up and down the rocky mountainsides. Instead of having hooves like goats or horses, llamas have feet with two toes on each foot. Wide pads, much like a dog's, cover the bottom of them. The pads make it possible for the llamas to feel the ground under their feet.

Because llamas have soft feet, they don't damage the soil or plants as cattle do.

Diet

Llamas don't need as much water as cattle and sheep. Much of the water they get comes from the grass and shrubs that make up their diet.

Llamas have stomachs with three separate compartments. When they eat, the food goes down their *esophagus* (eh-SAH-fuh-gus) into the first compartment.

The partly chewed food comes back up into their mouth as *cud*. Cud is food that has been partly digested. More chewing

The <u>esophagus</u> is the tube that connects the mouth to the stomach.

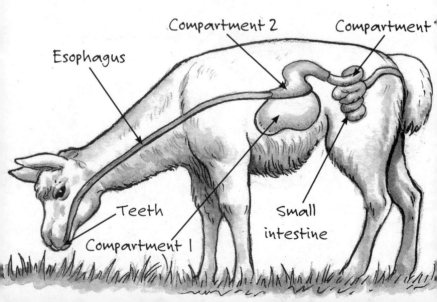

Compartment 2

Compartment

Esophagus

Teeth

Small intestine

Compartment 1

breaks down the food until it's soft enough to fully digest. Llamas chew their cud about eight hours a day!

Cows, deer, goats, sheep, and giraffes digest their food the same way.

Llamas often live in groups of twenty or more.

Behavior

Llamas are herd animals that like company. In fact, when a llama lives alone, it gets lonely and tries to connect with other animals. Sheep farmers have found that male llamas make good watchdogs.

If there are no other llamas around, they bond with the sheep and guard them against predators like coyotes and mountain lions. Sheep farmers usually have only one llama at a time with their flocks. If they used two, the llamas would hang out together and ignore the sheep!

In Switzerland, this llama protects sheep from wolves.

Crias

Llamas live to be about twenty or thirty years old. Females don't often mate until they are three. About a year later, they will have a baby llama, called a *cria* (KREE-uh).

As a mother gives birth, all the females stand guard to protect her from danger.

Crias usually nurse until they're about six months old.

Newborn llamas weigh over twenty-five pounds. They begin to walk and nurse when they are just a few hours old.

Cria nursing

Communication

Llamas have several ways of communicating. They often make humming or clucking sounds. A mother llama hums to her baby to let it know she is nearby. If llamas sense a predator, they warn the others with a high-pitched call or scream.

If a llama stands very straight and holds its head up high, it is on the alert for trouble. And if it folds its ears back flat, then watch out . . . it might start spitting!

If llamas are mad, they spit at other llamas to tell them to back off. And sometimes they aim at humans. Llamas can hit a target ten feet away. It's a bad idea to annoy a llama. But if you do, stand back at least eleven feet! Actually, you'd better make it twelve!

Most llamas are gentle, intelligent animals that are comfortable around people. If someone overloads them, they don't spit, kick, or bite. Instead, they lie down and simply refuse to get up.

Llama owners say it is easy to train llamas. They are fast learners, and curious. If you ever get near a llama, it might walk over to sniff your face. This is how they get to know other llamas as well.

People attach colored threads to a llama's ears to identify it.

Because llamas are so important to them, the Aymara people of Peru and Bolivia call them their silent brothers. The ancient Incas honored these valuable animals by creating beautiful llama statues made of pure gold.

How to Meet and Greet a Llama

There are llama farms everywhere. If you visit one, it's good to know how to greet a llama.

First, let the llama come up to you. Don't be noisy or wave your hands around. Don't sing or whistle or jump up and down. Move slowly. And don't stare right into its eyes—the llama might feel threatened.

If the llama feels comfortable, it will sniff your face to get your scent. Otherwise, it will back away. Don't pat its head if it stays near you. Just try softly touching it on the sides of its neck.

3

Animals of the Andes

At least a thousand kinds of animal species live in the Andes. Many are not found anywhere else in the world. These animals live in specific habitats that are the best for them. Some prefer wet, warm areas, and others live in high deserts.

Many guanacos, for example, live in the dry plains of the central Andes. They roam the treeless land eating scrubby grasses while staying away from the rocks and cliffs of the high mountains. Foxes, skunks, and eagles also prefer this habitat.

Llamas and alpacas thrive at high altitudes. Medium-size taruca deer also prefer high altitudes. People have spotted them grazing at over 16,000 feet. When the weather gets cold, they head for lower ground.

Chinchillas also come from the high Andes. Their relatives appeared about

Today many people keep chinchillas as pets.

41 million years ago. They have thick fur to protect against the cold. In the wild, chinchillas jump from rock to rock. They can jump as high as six feet!

Another animal that exists at high altitudes is the beautiful Andean mountain cat. This small cat often lives alone in the high, dry parts of the mountains. The cats are rarely seen, and researchers know little about their habits. They are an endangered species—only about 2,500 remain. Unlike other animals of the Andes, no Andean mountain cats are living in captivity.

Most people think pink flamingos only live in wetlands and lakes where the weather is warm. Some of the most beautiful flamingos, however, live in the cool wetlands and lakes of the Andes.

Andean flamingos

Huge flocks of as many as 1,000 Andean flamingos poke around in the lakes and wetlands, looking for algae to eat. They can survive at over 11,000 feet but move to lower ground when it gets too cold.

An amazing frog as small as the tip of your thumb has been discovered in a cloud forest in Ecuador. What's truly strange about this tiny creature is that it can change its skin from spiky to smooth in only a few minutes. This quick change helps the frogs disguise themselves when danger approaches.

Come on! Let's look for more animals in the Andes!

Jaguars

Jaguars are the largest predators in the Andes and throughout North and South America. Only lions and tigers are bigger. Jaguars have markings that look like a leopard's. These powerful animals can be nine feet long, including their tail, and weigh up to 300 pounds.

Jaguars are meat eaters that can take down animals weighing much more than they do. This is possible because their jaws are stronger than a lion's! In fact, a jaguar's jaws are so powerful that they can easily bite through the tough hide of a crocodile.

Jaguars often live near swamps and in areas with trees. They can swim across rivers and lakes. Their great swimming skills help them catch turtles and fish that they sometimes eat underwater!

Spectacled Bears

The cloud forests of Peru are home to the rare spectacled bear. These medium-size animals are the only bear in the Andes. They are very shy, so people almost never see them.

Spectacled bears have white or light tan fur on the sides of their nose and above their eyes. They got their name because they look as if they're wearing spectacles, or eyeglasses.

The bears build platforms made of vines and branches high in the trees. They eat and sleep there most of the day. Although they sometimes eat meat, they mainly live on plants. If they get really hungry, they'll even eat cacti.

Andean Condors

Condors are the largest flying birds in the world. They weigh about thirty-three pounds, and have a wingspan around ten feet across. Condors live at altitudes of 9,000 to 16,000 feet.

Condors can travel 120 miles a day! Because their bodies are so heavy, they save energy by soaring along with the wind currents.

Condors belong to the vulture family and eat the meat from dead animals. They can eat several pounds and then go days without any food at all. The Incas believed that these great birds were messengers from the gods.

Pumas

Puma is another name for mountain lions, or cougars. They live in both North and South America. Pumas are the fourth-largest cats in the world. They are almost eight feet from the end of their tail to the tip of their nose.

Pumas prey on large animals, like deer and livestock. Since they can run fifty miles per hour and can jump fifteen feet, they are deadly predators.

When pumas make a kill, they usually eat part of it and save the rest by dragging it under leaves or sticks. Pumas and condors often fight over the leftovers. And a lot of times the pumas lose!

Vizcachas

Vizcachas look like fat rabbits with big bushy tails. They are actually rodents, like hamsters, mice, and rats, and are closely related to chinchillas. They live in colonies and have their burrows in the rocks.

Vizcachas are social and communicate their feelings through sound. They grunt, squeal loudly, moan, and at times make noises together in a chorus. If a predator comes around, the animals make a whistling noise that sounds like a birdcall. It means "Hide!"

To hide, vizcachas can jump quickly from rock to rock. They are so fast that predators have a hard time following.

Andean Hairy Armadillos

Because this animal looks like a small knight in armor, the Spanish called it an armadillo, which means "little armored one." An armadillo's armor is the bony shell on its back.

In the Andes, armadillos sprout hair from beneath their shell and on their bodies and legs. They have strong, short legs. But these short legs help them run at speeds of up to thirty miles per hour!

Armadillos use their sharp front claws to dig burrows and tunnels. Some are so wide and deep that they ruin the foundations of houses.

Millions of years ago, ancient relatives of armadillos were huge—ten feet long and weighing a ton! Just think of what *their* burrows were like!

4

The Incas

People have lived in the Andes for thousands of years. Early Andean people practiced their own customs, languages, and religions. Although some lived in cities, most were farmers, growing crops on the steep mountain slopes. They raised llamas and wove their wool into beautiful clothes just as many Andeans do today.

A people known as the *Incas* settled in

the Cuzco Valley of Peru. Inca legends say their ancestors first came to the valley about 800 years ago. They made the city of Cuzco their capital.

With the help of a skilled army, the Incas defeated most of the tribes in what is now Peru, Bolivia, Chile, Ecuador, and Argentina. They took control of the land and ruled the people who lived there.

By 1500, the Inca Empire was very powerful. From his palace in Cuzco, the Inca emperor ruled about 40,000 of his fellow Incas and up to 12 million people from other tribes.

The empire stretched over 2,500 miles and was one of the largest empires in history.

Language

The Incas spoke a language called *Quechua* (KEH-chuh-wuh). Quechua became the official language of the empire, although many people in the southern part spoke Aymara.

Quechua is still one of the three main languages in South America, along with Spanish and Portuguese. More than 7 million people speak some form of the language.

Today Cuzco's Plaza de Armas is a popular place for tourists and Peruvians to gather.

Cuzco

Mountains surround Cuzco. This was where Inca nobles, their servants, and other workers lived. During the Inca Empire, about 40,000 people lived in Cuzco.

Cuzco was a beautiful city with narrow streets. There were fountains, palaces, temples, and shrines. Water from two rivers filled the canals that ran through the city.

Most of Cuzco's buildings were made of stone blocks. Many weighed several tons. In fact, there are huge stones in a fortress near Cuzco that weigh over a hundred tons!

The buildings were strong because the Incas were very skilled stonecutters. The stone blocks in buildings

66

The fortress is called Sacsayhuamán.

and walls fit together perfectly without cement or mortar to keep them in place. Workers built ramps to move the stones into place without any modern tools or equipment. Using only simple hand tools like stone hammers, the Incas managed to create very strong buildings that remained standing during many powerful earthquakes.

Inca noblemen wore big gold ear ornaments.

The Emperor and His Government

People believed the Sapa Inca, or emperor, had a special link to Inti, the sun god. Everyone obeyed the emperor without question. Because of his connection to the sun, the Inca nobility called themselves "children of the sun."

The emperor had many wives, but the main one was called the *Coya*. She and the emperor worked closely together, building palaces and managing their estates. The Coya was in charge of special religious houses where women priests lived.

There were male and female priests.

In the main sun temple in Cuzco, specially chosen women slept in a room with a statue of the sun. They put clothes on the statue, cooked food for it, and took it out on the patio every day!

The emperor and empress were carried around on litters like this.

69

The emperor and his family lived in a splendid palace. They ate and drank from gold and silver plates and cups. Each new emperor built his own palace.

Inca emperors wore beautiful clothes and jewelry made of fine gold and silver. Even the women's hats had gold trim. There are stories that the emperors wore their clothes only once and then had them burned!

Great Weavers

In Cuzco, women priests known as Mothers lived in special houses called the houses of the chosen ones. The Incas chose beautiful young girls to be trained by the Mothers. The women taught the girls how to weave and prepare food and drinks for religious ceremonies. The

This Inca poncho shows the complex patterns of the weaving.

Mothers were such expert weavers that they were the only people allowed to make the emperor's clothes.

Ceremonies and Funerals

When there was an important ceremony, the emperor sat on a great throne on a raised platform.

After an emperor or empress died, their body was mummified. At the funeral, people danced and told stories about how great they were. Afterward, the priests returned the mummy to the palace.

They burned food on special fires for the mummy to "eat." Servants sat next to it, waving fans to keep the flies away!

When there were parades and festivals, people carried the mummy through the streets.

Managing the Empire

The emperor spent much of his time caring for the empire. In order to control his lands, he divided the empire into four areas. His closest male relatives were in charge of the different sections and reported back to the emperor.

Llama caravan on the move!

The empire was connected by more than 14,000 miles of roads and hundreds of bridges. Llama caravans often traveled the roads, carrying goods all over the empire. It wasn't unusual to see a hundred llamas or more in a caravan!

Some ancient Inca roads still exist today.

Government officials traveled the roads as well. Because they were in service to the emperor, there were lodgings for them along the way stocked with food, water, and clothing.

Mail Delivery

When the emperor sent messages to different parts of his empire, teams of young men who were skilled runners acted as messengers. The men lived in the same shelters along the road that government workers used. Since the Incas had no writing, the runners memorized the messages.

The emperor commands you to bring more fish to his palace in Cuzco!

One runner would run six to nine miles from his hut to the next and pass the message to a runner there. A team of good runners could cover 150 miles a day!

Keeping Records

Incas didn't have a written language. Specially trained officials recorded information on *quipus* (KEE-pooz). These were cotton or wool cords with more colored strings attached to them. The strings were tied into knots, which acted as a kind of code that stood for numbers.

Some large quipus had over 1,000 strings!

The government used quipus to keep track of things like how many llamas and alpacas there were in an area or how many potatoes were in a warehouse.

Temple of the Sun

The most important building in Cuzco was the Temple of the Sun in the center of town. The four main roads in the empire came together nearby.

Four thousand priests lived in the temple.

The walls were lined with gold and silver. The roof straw was coated with gold so it would shine brightly in the sunlight.

The temple had incredible gardens, with sculptures of flowers, insects, corn, birds, and other animals. Some stories told about gold statues of llamas in the gardens. The temple must have been an amazing sight!

This gold figurine of a llama shows how important llamas were to the Incas.

Gods and Spirits

The Incas had many gods. Besides the sun god, others included the thunder god, the god of the rain, the earth mother, and the goddess of the moon. There were also spirits called *Apus* that were connected to the mountains. The Incas believed that each mountain had a special spirit to protect the crops and animals.

At night, the Incas looked at a constellation called *Urcuchillay*. They imagined Urcuchillay looked like a llama of many colors and took it as a sign that their animals were protected.

An Inca myth said that llamas once spoke to two shepherds to warn them that a great flood was coming. The shepherds took their families and animals

high up into the mountains. It rained for months, but then the sun god appeared and the sun returned. Ever since, the myth claims, llamas have lived high in the mountains to keep themselves safe from floods.

The Incas held religious festivals and feasts to celebrate a good harvest, especially of corn. They also had them for protection from earthquakes, floods, and *droughts*. Some festivals lasted for days. One of the most important was held on the shortest day of the year.

A <u>drought</u> (DROWT) is a time of very little rain.

Inca Farmers

Most Incas lived in small villages. They shared the land and worked together, growing beans, quinoa (KEEN-wah),

squash, and fruit. They also raised corn
and many kinds of potatoes. There were
warehouses all over the empire where the
emperor had them store food, wool, and
other supplies in case of an emergency.

The Incas had a way of drying

potatoes so they could eat them later. They also dried meat to preserve it. The Quechua word for dried meat is _ch'arki_.

Besides llamas and alpacas, the only animals farmers kept were Muscovy ducks and guinea pigs. Many South Americans eat guinea pigs today!

The sides of the mountains were so steep that it was hard for crops to grow there. To solve this problem, farmers dug long, flat steps called _terraces_ across the slopes. They filled them with dirt, sand, and gravel. Stone walls supported the terraces and stopped the crops from washing away.

People used stone stairways to get from one terrace to another.

To give plants enough water in the rocky, thin soil of the Andes, people built miles of stone canals that carried water to the fields.

82

The terraces' stone walls stored heat during the day and kept plants from freezing at night.

End of the Empire

In the 1520s, Spanish explorers arrived, bringing diseases that killed many Incas, including the emperor. For four years, the Incas fought with each other for control of the empire.

In 1532, the Spanish killed the new emperor and attacked Inca towns and forts. By 1572, Spain had conquered the once-great Inca Empire. It had lasted just over one hundred years.

The Incas had created a great nation and a strong government without the use of wheels, horses, writing, or machinery. Over the years, ruins of Inca buildings remained hidden in the mountains, smothered by jungle vines and worn away by time.

Potatoes and Clay!

For thousands of years, people in the Andes have eaten different kinds of potatoes. Some of them taste bitter, and used to make them sick. It turns out that certain wild potatoes have natural toxins in them.

Researchers were curious to know why natives from the high plateau areas of the Andes ate their potatoes with a sauce called *chaco*. It is made of water, salt, and clay. They analyzed the clay and found that it contained minerals that pulled out the toxins from the potatoes.

People in the Andes learned to soak potatoes to get rid of the toxins and the bitter taste. Some Andeans still practice the old way of eating their potatoes, with chaco.

5

Machu Picchu

In 1911, an American history professor and explorer named Hiram Bingham arrived in Cuzco. Hiram was loaded down with cameras, tents, maps, and notebooks. He had come to find the lost Inca city of Vilcabamba, the last city held by the Incas before their defeat by the Spanish in 1572.

No one knew exactly where Vilcabamba was. Before the Spanish attacked, the Incas burned much of the city to the ground. Hiram had heard that its ruins might be in the mountains outside Cuzco.

The Adventure Begins

Hiram and his team set off, first on mules, and then on foot. He was in awe of the

Hiram Bingham, 1912

towering mountain peaks, canyons, and thick jungles. The men camped beside the roaring Urubamba River.

A farmer named Melchor Artega told Hiram about ruins on top of a nearby mountain called *Machu Picchu* (MATCH-oo PEEK-choo).

Machu Picchu means "Old Mountain" in Quechua.

Hiram hired Melchor to guide him up the mountain. He grabbed his camera and tied thick cloth around his leather boots for protection against a deadly snake called the *fer-de-lance*.

The fer-de-lance is the most dangerous snake in South America.

When the men left camp, it was pouring. They struggled up the mountain for about two hours, until they came to a simple hut where a farm family lived.

People there welcomed Hiram with some sweet potatoes and cool water. The farmer told his young son to take Hiram

Hiram Bingham took this picture of the outer wall of Machu Picchu.

Ten-foot-tall stone walls support the terraces.

up the mountain to Machu Picchu.

The boy guided Hiram as they clambered up the slippery, steep terraces covered in vines, trees, and moss. As they got close to the top, Hiram had counted at least one hundred terraces connected by stairways.

Machu Picchu

When he got to Machu Picchu, Hiram saw the vine-covered ruins of buildings made of granite. Many of the roofs had fallen in, but he could see that this had once been a magnificent place.

He took notes on the temples, fountains, palaces, and houses. Hiram later

wrote to his wife, saying that Machu Picchu was so beautiful, it took his breath
away.

Hiram stayed at Machu Picchu only
one day. He left feeling absolutely certain he'd discovered the lost city of Vilcabamba. (He was wrong!)

Return to Machu Picchu

Hiram returned to Machu Picchu in 1912.
With him was a team of *archaeologists*
(ar-kee-AH-luh-jists) and other workers.
Archaeologists learn about people from
the past by studying things they left be-
hind, like buildings, tools, jewelry, and
human remains.

When they reached Machu Picchu,
workers began hacking through the
thick jungle vines, cane, and trees to see

what was underneath. In all, it took four months to clear the growth that covered the site.

At last Hiram and the team saw where narrow streets, temples, palaces, and houses had been. The men made maps, and Hiram took about 200 pictures.

This is one of Hiram's photos of Machu Picchu after all the work.

Stonework

The Incas used stone that was already there to build Machu Picchu. But teams of Inca workers also pushed large boulders up the steep mountain slopes. Then they chiseled, or carved, them into the shapes they needed.

The stones fit together so perfectly that even a thin knife blade couldn't be pushed between them.

Vilcabamba or What?

Once again, Hiram left believing that he'd found Vilcabamba, the great lost city of the Incas. Today we know that the ruins of Vilcabamba lie deep in the jungle, about one hundred miles west of Cuzco. The strange thing is that Hiram had actually seen these ruins before but didn't think they were important!

Hiram wrote about his adventures. He believed for the rest of his life that Machu Picchu was Vilcabamba. But thanks to his writings, people all over the world learned about the wonderful hidden world of Machu Picchu.

Machu Picchu After Hiram

Researchers have spent many years studying Machu Picchu. They've discovered much more about the site. They've even made 3-D computer models of it.

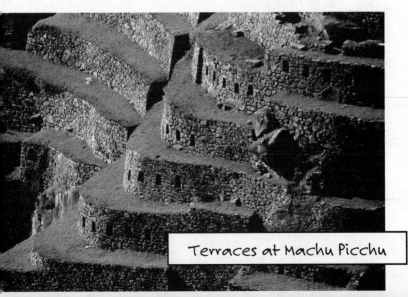

Terraces at Machu Picchu

There are bathhouses and a prison among the buildings.

Machu Picchu is truly a place of wonder. It sits almost 8,000 feet above sea level. There are over 600 terraces and about 200 buildings. Among them are clusters of houses, temples, and plazas.

And there are lots and lots of steps! The main street is one long staircase. There are also a hundred other stairways. In all, Machu Picchu has 3,000 steps!

Sixteen fountains bringing water from a stream were spaced up and down the main stairway. People filled pitchers from them.

Fountain from Machu Picchu

In 1990, workers cleared dirt from a fountain and a canal. They were startled that after so many years, water flowed out of both of them!

What Was Machu Picchu?

Archaeologists say that Machu Picchu wasn't really a city at all. Some think it was a summer retreat, or vacation spot, where the emperor and other nobles got away to relax. Other archaeologists believe it was for religious ceremonies.

Only about 300 to 1,000 people ever lived in Machu Picchu. Many were nobles, highly skilled workers, or servants. After the Spanish destroyed the empire, the Incas abandoned Machu Picchu forever. The buildings fell into ruins and were swallowed up by the jungle.

Today Machu Picchu is a popular place to visit. No one lives there, and when the tourists go home at night, the llamas and alpacas have this ancient place all to themselves.

Hiram Takes Precious Objects

Hiram got permission from the government of Peru to take thousands of objects from Machu Picchu back to the United States. Among them were broken bits of pottery, tools, and the skulls and other bones of bodies he discovered in tombs. Hiram sent everything he found to Yale University, where he was teaching. Yale put them in its museum.

It is now against the law to take objects from ancient sites. Peru asked Yale to return the objects Hiram had taken. By 2012, the university had sent them all back. They had been out of Peru for one hundred years. Today they are in a museum in Cuzco.

6

The Old and New

In the Andes today, the old and new live side by side. In fact, the past and present fit together as tightly as Inca stonework. About one-third of the people in South America live in the cities and villages of the Andes.

About half of the people living in the Andes have Inca ancestors. Quite a few of them live very much as their relatives lived.

Farming Today

Farmers still grow many of the same things. Potatoes are their biggest crop, but the tomatoes we eat today began as wild tomatoes in the Andes thousands of years ago!

Almost every supermarket in the U.S. sells quinoa. People in the Andes cultivated it 5,000 years ago. Quinoa is rich in protein, vitamins, and minerals.

Most farming families are Christian, but many still make offerings to the earth and pray to the mountains as their Inca ancestors did.

Farmers are bringing back the old Inca way of watering their crops. The government of Peru has begun a program to restore the canals and terraces that Andeans built 3,000 years ago.

The Andes are so steep that farmers still can't use most modern farm machinery. But llamas and alpacas are no longer the only large animals on their farms. Some have begun raising cattle and sheep.

Tourists Flock to the Andes

People often take vacations in the Andes. Cuzco has over three million visitors a year! Many come to visit the Inca ruins. There are national parks where hikers can see unique animals and plants. Mountain climbers tackle some of the highest peaks in the world.

Torres del Paine National Park

Aconcagua is the tallest mountain outside Asia.

Thousands of people climb Mount Aconcagua every year. The easiest route calls for eighteen to twenty days of hard climbing!

Machu Picchu and Other Ruins

Over the years, archaeologists have found ruins in the Andes that few people knew existed. It wasn't until 1969 that they began work on Vilcabamba and uncovered what was left of the palace. It had a huge main hall with twenty-six doors and many streets and stairways.

Machu Picchu is now a national park. It is such an important place that the United Nations declared it a World Heritage Site in 1983.

World Heritage Sites, like the Statue of Liberty, are protected from destruction or change.

Visitors pay to get in. People must stay on the paths so nothing is damaged, and they can only visit for four hours.

Some llamas and alpacas still live among the ruins of Machu Picchu.

Llamas Today

People all over the world now own llamas. They are so popular, they're in books, movies, TV commercials, and cartoons.

 There are even llama pillows, clothes, and towels.

Most llamas in the United States are pets. But some are also working animals. They can be guards or pack animals, and some people sell their wool, although alpaca wool is more valuable.

Rojo

Llamas can also be trained to be therapy animals. Rojo (ROH-ho) is probably the

most famous therapy llama ever. He visits hospitals, schools, and nursing homes in the northwest United States. Because he's such a gentle creature, people feel good being with him. They call Rojo the world's most beloved llama. He even has his own Facebook page!

People getting married outdoors in Oregon can rent llamas to be in their weddings!

When you think about the role llamas have played in the history of the Andes, it's not surprising that people all over the world have heard about these incredible animals. After all, one of the greatest empires the world has ever known would not have existed without the help of llamas.

Doing More Research

There's a lot more you can learn about llamas and the Andes. The fun of research is seeing how many different sources you can explore.

Books

Most libraries and bookstores have books about llamas, the Incas, and the Andes.

Here are some things to remember when you're using books for research:

1. You don't have to read the whole book. Check the table of contents and the index to find the topics you're interested in.

2. Write down the name of the book.

When you take notes, make sure you write down the name of the book in your note-book so you can find it again.

3. Never copy exactly from a book.

When you learn something new from a book, put it in your own words.

4. Make sure the book is <u>nonfiction</u>.

Some books tell make-believe stories about llamas and the Andes. Make-believe stories are called *fiction*. They're fun to read, but not good for research.

Research books have facts and tell true stories. They are called *nonfiction*. A librarian or teacher can help you make sure the books you use for research are non-fiction.

Here are some good nonfiction books about llamas and the Andes:

- *The Andes* by Molly Aloian
- *The Inca Empire* (A True Book) by Sandra Newman
- *Llamas* by Mary R. Dunn
- *Llamas* (DK Readers Level 2) by Laura Buller
- *Llamas* (Living Wild) by Melissa Gish
- *Llamas* (A True Book) by Emilie U. Lepthien
- *This Place Is High* by Vicki Cobb
- *Where Is Machu Picchu?* by Megan Stine

Museums

Many museums can help you learn more about llamas, the Incas, and the Andes.

When you go to a museum:

1. Be sure to take your notebook!
Write down anything that catches your interest. Draw pictures, too!

2. Ask questions.
There are almost always people at museums who can help you find what you're looking for.

3. Check the calendar.
Many museums have special events and activities just for kids!

Here are some museums where you can learn about the Incas and the Andes:

- American Museum of Natural History (New York)
- Peabody Museum of Natural History (New Haven, CT)
- Smithsonian National Museum of the American Indian (Washington, D.C.)

There are zoos and llama farms in almost every state. Here are a few:

- Lincoln Children's Zoo (Lincoln, NE)
- Long Island Game Farm (Manorville, NY)
- Denver Zoo (Colorado)
- San Diego Zoo (San Diego)

The Internet

Many websites have lots of facts about llamas, the Incas, and the Andes. Some also have activities that can help make learning about llamas, the Incas, and the Andes easier.

Ask your teacher or your parents to help you find more websites like these:

- incas.mrdonn.org
- kids.kiddle.co/Machu_Picchu
- kids.nationalgeographic.com/explore /countries/peru
- kids.sandiegozoo.org/animals/andean-bear
- nationalgeographic.com/animals /mammals/l/llama
- scienceforkidsclub.com/machu-picchu

Bibliography

Bingham, Hiram. *Lost City of the Incas.* New York: Phoenix Press, 2002.

Hemming, John. *Conquest of the Incas.* Boston: Houghton Mifflin Harcourt, 2012.

Jacobs, Michael. *Andes.* Berkeley: Counterpoint, 2011.

Malpass, Michael A. *Ancient People of the Andes.* Ithaca: Cornell University Press, 2016.

McGee, Marty. *Llamas and Alpacas as a Metaphor for Life.* Bend, OR: Raccoon Press, 2003.

Sullivan, William. *The Secret of the Incas.* New York: Random House, 1996.

Index

Have you read the adventure that matches up with this book?

Don't miss

Magic Tree House® #34

LATE LUNCH WITH LLAMAS

When the magic tree house whisks Jack and Annie to the Andes, they find a boy whose baby llama has been stolen. Can Jack and Annie climb to the peak of Machu Picchu to complete this rescue mission?

Magic Tree House®

#1: DINOSAURS BEFORE DARK
#2: THE KNIGHT AT DAWN
#3: MUMMIES IN THE MORNING
#4: PIRATES PAST NOON
#5: NIGHT OF THE NINJAS
#6: AFTERNOON ON THE AMAZON
#7: SUNSET OF THE SABERTOOTH
#8: MIDNIGHT ON THE MOON
#9: DOLPHINS AT DAYBREAK
#10: GHOST TOWN AT SUNDOWN
#11: LIONS AT LUNCHTIME
#12: POLAR BEARS PAST BEDTIME
#13: VACATION UNDER THE VOLCANO
#14: DAY OF THE DRAGON KING
#15: VIKING SHIPS AT SUNRISE
#16: HOUR OF THE OLYMPICS
#17: TONIGHT ON THE *TITANIC*
#18: BUFFALO BEFORE BREAKFAST
#19: TIGERS AT TWILIGHT
#20: DINGOES AT DINNERTIME
#21: CIVIL WAR ON SUNDAY
#22: REVOLUTIONARY WAR ON WEDNESDAY
#23: TWISTER ON TUESDAY
#24: EARTHQUAKE IN THE EARLY MORNING
#25: STAGE FRIGHT ON A SUMMER NIGHT
#26: GOOD MORNING, GORILLAS
#27: THANKSGIVING ON THURSDAY
#28: HIGH TIDE IN HAWAII
#29: A BIG DAY FOR BASEBALL
#30: HURRICANE HEROES IN TEXAS
#31: WARRIORS IN WINTER
#32: TO THE FUTURE, BEN FRANKLIN!
#33: NARWHALS ON A SUNNY NIGHT
#34: LATE LUNCH WITH LLAMAS

Magic Tree House® Merlin Missions

#1: CHRISTMAS IN CAMELOT
#2: HAUNTED CASTLE ON HALLOWS EVE
#3: SUMMER OF THE SEA SERPENT
#4: WINTER OF THE ICE WIZARD
#5: CARNIVAL AT CANDLELIGHT
#6: SEASON OF THE SANDSTORMS
#7: NIGHT OF THE NEW MAGICIANS
#8: BLIZZARD OF THE BLUE MOON
#9: DRAGON OF THE RED DAWN
#10: MONDAY WITH A MAD GENIUS
#11: DARK DAY IN THE DEEP SEA
#12: EVE OF THE EMPEROR PENGUIN
#13: MOONLIGHT ON THE MAGIC FLUTE
#14: A GOOD NIGHT FOR GHOSTS
#15: LEPRECHAUN IN LATE WINTER
#16: A GHOST TALE FOR CHRISTMAS TIME
#17: A CRAZY DAY WITH COBRAS
#18: DOGS IN THE DEAD OF NIGHT
#19: ABE LINCOLN AT LAST!
#20: A PERFECT TIME FOR PANDAS
#21: STALLION BY STARLIGHT
#22: HURRY UP, HOUDINI!
#23: HIGH TIME FOR HEROES
#24: SOCCER ON SUNDAY
#25: SHADOW OF THE SHARK
#26: BALTO OF THE BLUE DAWN
#27: NIGHT OF THE NINTH DRAGON

Magic Tree House®
Super Edition

#1: WORLD AT WAR, 1944

Magic Tree House®
Fact Trackers

<table>
<tr><td>

Dinosaurs
Knights and Castles
Mummies and Pyramids
Pirates
Rain Forests
Space
Titanic
Twisters and Other Terrible Storms
Dolphins and Sharks
Ancient Greece and the Olympics
American Revolution
Sabertooths and the Ice Age
Pilgrims
Ancient Rome and Pompeii
Tsunamis and Other Natural Disasters
Polar Bears and the Arctic
Sea Monsters
Penguins and Antarctica
Leonardo da Vinci
Ghosts
Leprechauns and Irish Folklore
Rags and Riches: Kids in the Time of
   Charles Dickens
Snakes and Other Reptiles
Dog Heroes
Abraham Lincoln

</td><td>

Pandas and Other Endangered Species
Horse Heroes
Heroes for All Times
Soccer
Ninjas and Samurai
China: Land of the Emperor's Great
   Wall
Sharks and Other Predators
Vikings
Dogsledding and Extreme Sports
Dragons and Mythical Creatures
World War II
Baseball
Wild West
Texas
Warriors
Benjamin Franklin
Narwhals and Other Whales
Llamas and the Andes

</td></tr>
</table>

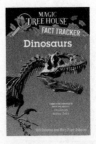

More Magic Tree House®

Games and Puzzles from the Tree House
Magic Tricks from the Tree House
My Magic Tree House Journal
Magic Tree House Survival Guide
Animal Games and Puzzles
Magic Tree House Incredible Fact Book